FROM MY WEAKNESS TO HIS STRENGTH

Exchanging Our Weakness

For God's Strength

Dennis Paul Goldsworthy-Davis

Open Wells Ministries

7995 Heuermann Rd

San Antonio, TX 78256

www.openwellsministries.org

Library of Congress Number:

ISBN: 978-1-7355716-7-6

Printed in the United States of America by Open Wells Ministries

Contents

There is not a one of us who doesn't have a sense of our own frailty. When I say frailty, I am not speaking of a physical infirmity, even though that can apply. I am speaking of the weakness of our flesh. Jesus said in admonishing His disciples to pray, *that the spirit was willing but the flesh was weak.* The *flesh* was a reference to our *carnal* nature that all of us have and war against. We are in a constant battle against this nature. The Apostle Paul gave us insight into this conflict that we all as believers are engaged in.

> *"For the flesh lusts against the Spirit, and the Spirit against the flesh; and these are contrary to one another, so that you do not do the things that you wish."*
> Galatians 5:17

The desire and will of the Holy Spirit in our lives is being fought against by this *flesh* that is referred to. This can produce in us a sense of weakness and inability. There is a desire in us to do the will of God, yet there are other desires that fight against this. The critical key to which desire wins is the *choice* we make. This is where we need to go from weakness to strength. This happens through the *spirit of might* operating in us. Ephesians 3:16 speaks of this strength that comes to us from *might* being imparted in our most inward places.

"... that He would grant you, according to the riches of His glory, to be strengthened with might through His Spirit in the inner man..." Ephesians 3:16

The word *might* in this scripture is the Greek word *dunamis.* It means *a force, a miraculous power, an ability or strength.* Notice that this *might* is in the inner man. We are strengthened through a supernatural encounter with the power of God. This power that is imparted into our spirit, strengthens us to make the choices necessary to agree with God. We should never minimize this occurrence. Prior to this might and power being infused in our spirit, we have no ability to make these choices. However, when we are *strengthened with might in the inner man,* we now have the ability to choose and obey the mandates and dictates of God.

In this book *From Weakness to Strength,* this issue and others are addressed. We cannot do anything about the weaknesses associated with our humanity. These are universally true. However we can, through the power and might of the Spirit of God, move from these weaknesses to the strength and power of the Lord. Dennis helps us to understand but also receive impartation for this happening.

Weakness of the flesh does not have to dominate our lives, however it may manifest. There is a place in God where we can move from that weakness into the strength and power of our God. When this occurs, the frailty that once dominated and dictated our lives is broken. Instead of us being ruled over by cruel powers, we receive a power and anointing that allows us to rule instead. It is the glory and majesty of the grace of God to move us from servants to these things to masters operating in the power and might of who Jesus is. This is when we go from strength unto strength, faith unto faith and glory unto glory. We become a demonstration of His grace in the earth. When we come to the realization that we are nothing and can do nothing without Him, His might will infuse us to be the overcomers we were always intended to be!

Robert Henderson
Best-Selling Author of *The Court of Heaven* Series

One of my favorite scriptures for its pure revelation is when the Lord spoke to Abraham. His promise to him was whatever he saw would be his and his descendants.

> *"...Look around you from where you are.... I will give you all the land you see. I will give it forever to you and your family."* Genesis 13:15

In other words, truth has to be seen and when it is seen it can be owned. This book is as a result of a truth that I personally have seen and started to own in an ever-increasing manner. In fact, the Lord told me that the message in this book would be one of my life-long messages. It would be one of my messages that I would always carry. It is my joy to share this message with you. It is the message of God turning our weakness into his glorious strength!

The message was birthed in me due to an experience which I will try my best to relate to you in this introduction. Several years ago I was due to minister in several meetings in Connecticut and was flying from San Antonio through to Hartford when suddenly I contracted some strange sickness and had to stop in a hotel in Chicago. I spent a day and night there and had 24 hours of fevers and chills which accompanied the sickness. It left me so physically weak, indeed it did. It was one of those fevers that just took most of one's strength, but I was due to speak in Connecticut that next night and so dutifully I went. The ministry went well and despite me, the presence of God began to be released. The whole church ran forward for prayer and it was not a small church. Gosh! I was already weak but after that I dragged myself back to the hotel crying to myself and to the Lord for help.

The next day I drove to another part of the state and had two days of ministry. After the first night, the leader told me, "Everybody wants to be ministered to tomorrow". I was just not recovering from whatever had taken my strength. I remember taking a bath and crying out in my weakened state when suddenly a song started to be sung in my spirit. The song itself had supernatural foundations as the writer had heard it from an angel. These were the words: "In times of weakness, in times of storm, just lift your hands and praise the Lord."

The song sang over and over in my spirit and I cried out, "I receive that! I need that!" The next 30 minutes became shocking as wave after wave of the presence of God touched me. It was difficult to drive to the meeting as his presence overwhelmed me! As for the meeting? Oh, what glory touched the people! There were people literally crying out and shaking under his presence.

What had just happened? An incredible revelation had been released to me! The revelation that Paul had received:

The word *power [strength]* there is the word *Dunamis*. He had released his glorious *Dunamis* power to me in my weakness and has done so ever since.

A little later in prayer the Lord said these words to me: "This truth will be one of your life messages." It surely has become one to me as I have experienced this transforming revelation personally again and again. This book is my response to my heavenly mandate. FROM WEAKNESS TO STRENGTH. There is a world of revelation and empowering of the Lord waiting to be unlocked!!! The scripture says,

"Finally, be strong in the Lord and in his mighty power." Ephesians 6:10

This statement both seems to be a command and a conclusion. We must learn how to become people of His strength! I believe, in order to do so, the revelation that we will find in this book will help incredibly! May the journey begin!

CHAPTER 1

The Journey Begins

There is no message or book that can be written on weakness to strength without speaking of the power and glory of salvation. We know that weakness has within it the sense of moral weakness as well as every other aspect.

> *"But he said to me, 'My grace is sufficient for you*
> *for my power is made perfect in weakness.'."*
> 2 Corinthians 12:9

Quite simply we are powerless to change ourselves or save ourselves, yet the Lord will take the weakness of our lost state to pour his power of salvation … life changing salvation … into us and give us a new beginning touch by his grace and strength.

From the age of 1 day old to 15 years old my father took me and our family to church. I was moved by the messages of Jesus and clearly became a believer but was never touched by the power of salvation. I even went to confirmation classes in the Anglican Church, but no change came my way until I was invited to a Christian camp during my small journey within the military. I was clearly far from salvation even though a believer. I was a drunkard and violence was my lifestyle along with other iniquities. But what I saw at this camp began the journey of my clear conversion and my first taste of God's power to change us. People had definitely met God. Something had changed them. Some clearly glowed with the glory of God on their face. I was actually watching first-hand the famous Jesus movement. It wasn't too long before this touched me, though I yet had a journey to take.

It was January 1973 that I came fully face to face with the power of salvation. The Bible says,

> *"For I am not ashamed of the gospel, because it is the power of God that brings salvation to everyone!"* Romans 1:16

The power to take a life lost, weak in sin and depravity and transform it. I had stepped into a Pentecostal church because my wife to be went there to stop her mum from constantly asking her. Her father had met the Lord there about a year before. Now here I was, a long-haired tattooed hooligan, once again standing in the presence of God but, this time the power of conviction and the power of salvation hit me. It shook me and within several weeks I yielded my weak and lost life and felt his awesome forgiving power. I was wonderfully born again! Once again, I weep at the amazement of it all.

Yes, indeed, my first revelation of weakness to strength had been given to me to be followed by revelation after revelation in the days and years to come.

CHAPTER 2

Abraham The First to Teach Us
the Revelation of Weakness to Strength

Nobody can read the incredible story of Abraham without being able to see the awesome hand of God manifested in his life! The first manifestation of weakness turned into strength that we see! This is particularly important to us because we are given an incredible promise.

> *"So those who rely on faith are blessed along with Abraham, the man of faith."* Galatians 3:9

When we read such a promise it behooves us to want to examine every part of his life and what brought his blessing! Abraham's blessing came through his relationship with the Lord. Actually, he is called a friend of God.

> *"'But you, Israel, my servant,*
> *Jacob, whom I have chosen,*
> *you descendants of Abraham my friend...'"* Isaiah 41:8

We see this relationship not only in his constant communion with God but, also we see it in his obedience to God when told to move away from his home in Genesis 12. His faith in God's ability found in Romans 4 is an absolute key! He had faith that believed that despite his own weakness God would turn it to his own purpose. Abraham was the father who opened the door to weakness turned to strength. Let's discover what Romans tells us:

> *"As it is written: 'I have made you a father of many nations.'[1] He is our father in the sight of God, in whom he believed—the God who gives life to the dead and calls into being things that were not."*
> Romans 4:17

> *"Against all hope, Abraham in hope believed and so became the father of many nations."*
> Romans 8:18

> *"Without weakening in his faith, he faced the fact that his body was as good as dead-since he was about a hundred years old-and that Sarah's womb was also dead."* Romans 8:19

> *"Yet he did not waver through unbelief regarding the promise of God but was strengthened in his faith and gave glory to God."* Romans 8:20

> *"Being fully persuaded that God had power to do what he had promised."* Romans 4:21

It was this belief that released the awesome power of God to turn an old man who was beyond producing a child into a productive fruitful father.

Abraham teaches us to no longer rely on ourselves but on him who can do anything. He can take our absolute weakness and release his awesome strength. In fact, in Abraham's case, the Lord takes him to a place where he could no longer rely on himself because there was no self to rely on. *"A body as good as dead"* takes some beating but you also read that his wife had lost all hope in such a promise. In fact, she outwardly laughs when the Lord speaks of it.

> *"So Sarah laughed to herself as she thought, 'After I am worn out and my lord is old, will I now have this pleasure?'."* Genesis 18:12

In today's vernacular, "Oh sure! Oh really! Who are you kidding!" I guess she was just not in faith but that's what the Lord had turned up.

How did God do such a miraculous thing?

- ❖ By revealing the differing aspects of who he was! It started in Genesis 14:20 and went through to Genesis 17:1.

- ❖ By revealing destiny.
    - o *"So shall your offspring be!"* Genesis 15:5

- ❖ By stating his great promise more than once.
    - o *"But a son who is your own flesh and blood will be your heir."* Genesis 15:4

- ❖ By making covenant with Abraham.

- o *"To your descendants I will give this land."*
  Genesis15:18

❖ By changing Abraham's name from Abram to Abraham, from exalted father to father of a multitude thus releasing the seed of the supernatural into Abraham's life and walk.
  - o *"'No longer will you be called Abram[b]; your name will be Abraham, for I have made you a father of many nations.'"*
    Genesis 17:5

❖ By releasing the word of the Lord to Sarah and so releasing that same supernatural seed into her life. Awesome promise! That word should stir all up to believe!!
  - o *"'Is anything too hard for the Lord?'"*
    Genesis 18:14

Then comes the miracle! Was it gradual or sudden? Only heaven will reveal but I have my own take on it. One thing though is for sure, OUT OF WEAKNESS GOD DID A SUPERNATURAL MIRACLE AND TURNED THESE TWO TO STRENGTH IN AN AWESOME MANNER!

Let's state it again in a paraphrase: If we have faith alongside Abraham, we can be blessed alongside Abraham! If God did it with Abraham, he can and will do it for anyone who looks to him for his strength and promise.

CHAPTER 3

Go In The Strength That You Have

I love some of the conversations that we read of the Patriarchs when the Lord speaks beyond their experience or beyond their faith. One such conversation is found in Judges 6:11-16, when the Lord appears to Gideon. In this particular case I studied it in the NIV because of the way the words are phrased. It is no different from when the Lord changed Abram's name or Jacob's! This is how God sees it and how he sees you! God is speaking from his perspective not ours.

> *"When the angel of the Lord appeared to Gideon, he said, 'The Lord is with you, mighty warrior!'."*
> Judges 6:12

Now watch the answer! It is an instant deflection.

> *"'Pardon me, my lord,' Gideon replied, 'but if the Lord is with us, why has all this happened to us?'."*
> Judges 6:13

God is talking to Gideon, but Gideon deflects and brings Israel into it. He clearly doesn't see himself as the Lord sees him. The Lord sees a mighty warrior and Gideon sees a defeated people.

The conversation continues:

> *"The Lord turned to him and said, 'Go in the*
> *strength you have and save Israel out of Midian's*
> *hand. Am I not sending you?'*
> *'Pardon me, my Lord,' Gideon replied, 'but how*
> *can I save Israel? My clan is the weakest in*
> *Manasseh, and I am the least in my family.'."*
> Judges 6:13-15

Once again, two differing views. God's view and our view. Then came God's promise:

> *"The Lord answered, 'I will be with you…'."*
> Judges 6:16

AND HE WAS INDEED AS GIDEON OBEYED.

I could not leave this chapter out. Gideon saw his own weakness, but the Lord saw his future empowerment and spoke of it prophetically and creatively. Gideon had part of the equation right: I am weak, my family is weak and my clan is weak. YOU GOT THE WRONG GUY. The missing part was what God could do with a man open to his own weakness but allowing God's strength to come. You go in the strength you have and he will come in the strength he has!

FROM WEAKNESS TO STRENGTH! This came before Paul's revelation but this is the same God.

Our job is to be sober and real about ourselves but listen to what God sees and obey his prompting. His is not to ask for what we don't have but to allow what he has to step in the affray and journey. Time to start asking what he sees and what he wants us to do!

Church history as well as the Bible is so full of such stories. Yes, our God is a God who takes weakness and turns it to strength!

CHAPTER 4

Strengthened In the Inner Man

When we examine the power and life of the Spirit working with men, we recognize that he most often works within us even though many dramatic feats were done by his awesome power both in the Old and New Testaments. The scripture records him stirring us inwardly, praying through us and singing in us.

> *"So the Lord stirred up the spirit of Zerubbabel son of Shealtiel, governor of Judah, and the spirit of Joshua son of Jozadak, the high priest, and the spirit of the whole remnant of the people. They came and began to work on the house of the Lord Almighty, their God..."* Haggai 1:14

> *"In the same way, the Spirit helps us in our weakness. We do not know what we ought to pray for, but the Spirit himself intercedes for us through wordless groans."* Romans 8:26

> *"By day the Lord directs his love,*
> *at night his song is with me—*
> *a prayer to the God of my life."* Psalms 42:8

He creates thirst within and longing.

"You, God, are my God,
earnestly I seek you;

I thirst for you,
  my whole being longs for you,
in a dry and parched land
  where there is no water." Psalms 63:1

He envisions and directs us.

  "Deep calls to deep
    in the roar of your waterfalls;
  all your waves and breakers
    have swept over me." Psalm 42:7

  "'Do all that you have in mind,' his armor-bearer
  said. 'Go ahead; I am with you heart and soul.'"
  1 Samuel 14:7

The list could go on and on but, there is one thing that the
Holy Spirit does within us that is relative to this book, and
that is to:

  "...strengthen you with power through his Spirit in
  your inner being..." Ephesians 3:16

This scripture, in actual fact, comes from one of those
mighty prayers of Paul that is so revealing and inspiring.
He is praying that God would actually strengthen us out of
the riches of his glory by His Spirit, that he would actually
minister to our inner man from His place of glory and all
the wealth of it.

"I pray that he would grant you according to his riches in glory, to be strengthened with might through his Spirit in your inner man."
Ephesians 3:16 NKJV

But what is the reason? Not just so we could make it but, as scripture clearly tells us, that our inner man (our heart) is the key to life.

"Above all else, keep the heart for it is the wellspring of life." Proverbs 4:24 NIV 1984

As goes the heart, goes life. So, if our inner man (our heart) is continually strengthened by the Holy Spirit, the well spring flows in power and glory and revelation.

Coming back to Ephesians 3, in verses 17-20 we find out in its context that the reason for such strengthening is immense. Let's take it verse by verse.

"That Christ might dwell in your hearts through faith." Ephesians 3:17

"...being rooted and grounded in love"
Ephesians 3:17

That we would comprehend with all the saints the magnitude of this love:

"...may have power, together with all the Lord's holy people, to grasp how wide and long and high and deep is the love of Christ," Ephesians 3:18

THAT WE MIGHT BE FILLED WITH THE FULLNESS OF GOD:

"...and to know this love that surpasses knowledge—that you may be filled to the measure of all the fullness of God." Ephesians 3:19

In other words, strengthened so that we could comprehend and grasp and experience all that there is in God and to know it and be filled with all its great magnitude and power. But it doesn't stop there! There are two more verses in this passage that explain the magnitude of God's ability once he has brought us to such a place of fullness. Let's quote them in the original King James Version.

"Now unto him that is able to abundantly above all we can ask or think, according to the power that worketh within us, unto him be glory in the church." Ephesians 3:20-21 KJV

In summary, he strengthens from his glory so that when his love and fullness is released in us it glorifies him because his glory can be manifested fully. Surely we cry, "Strengthen us from your glory for your glory!".

There is another side to God's strengthening in the inner man that also bears mention.

"Do not be carried away by all kinds of strange teachings. It is good for our hearts to be strengthened by grace…" Hebrews 13:9

This scripture also has a three-fold chord to it, for within its context it actually says we aren't to be carried away by all kinds of strange teachings and to be so strengthened in our hearts that we can stand in his grace. This is chord number one!

The second chord to me is one of manifesting a praise that comes from a sacrificial heart, which becomes an open witness to him and of him.

"Through Jesus, therefore, let us continually offer to God a sacrifice of praise- the fruit of our lips that openly profess his name." Hebrews 13:15

The third chord is once more of sacrifice, the sacrifice of blessing others which in turn blesses God. There is a grace which once again enables and strengthens us beyond ourselves to stand and do what we could not normally do.

"And do not forget to do good and share with others, for with such sacrifices God is well pleased!" Hebrews 13:16

This strengthening can surely tie into Paul's great revelation:

When grace strengthens the heart and the inner man, things can be overcome, both from without and within. In context, Paul was able to stand against what had come against him from without, but I know how grace strengthened me so many times to defeat issues from within. I have actually written another book on this subject alone. Surely it is good for our hearts to be strengthened by Grace.

It makes you pray a second time, "Strengthen us, oh Lord, in the inner man we pray, IN EVERY DIMENSION and in every way.".

CHAPTER 5

Coming To the End of Yourself

Paul is shocked! He has just had a heavenly experience, literally caught up into the heavens and hearing inexpressible words, when a messenger of satan was sent to buffet him.

> *"Therefore, in order to keep me from becoming conceited, I was given a thorn in my flesh, a messenger of Satan, to torment me."*
> 2 Corinthians 12: 7

He must have thought, "What? How can this be? I have just been into the heavens and seen and heard amazing things, how can I be attacked now?"

The word *buffet* used here has within it the sense of one being on the ropes in a boxing ring and being punched and punched and punched continuously without a let up. But there is a warning in the context of Verse 7 which shows why the attack was so strong. He was in danger of self-exaltation or being exalted by others beyond what he should! This is a habit that we see too often in the body of Christ, I might add. It is seen both in the realm of ministry and in worship leaders. In fact, wherever there is success and a gift.

To add to Paul's misery, he had cried out to the Lord for deliverance three separate times and seemingly received no answer when suddenly, as we have pointed out, the Lord spoke making it clear that his grace is sufficient and his strength is made perfect in weakness.

Paul receives a shocking life-changing revelation, which may never have come unless he had suffered so. WHEN YOU ARE AT YOUR WEAKEST, HIS POWER AND GLORY IS AT ITS GREATEST! Why? Because you are no longer relying on your ability but his! It releases his grace to operate! No wonder the scripture says that blessed is the man whose strength is in God! Blessed because he has unlocked the key to what makes God's power operate. Today's western church is all about accomplishment and degrees and what man can do but, God's ways are all about what he can do when a man admits that his strength is in God!

Before we look at Paul's answer and response, we must look at what the word *weakness* means in this verse. It is the Greek word *Astheniah* which means *feebleness of mind and body*. It can also include *malady* and *moral frailty*. In any arena of weakness when we fall on his grace it can release his power at its greatest!

Paul's response is the key to this great truth.

> *"Therefore most gladly I will rather boast in my infirmities, that the power of Christ may rest upon me. Therefore I take pleasure in infirmities, in reproaches, in needs, in persecutions, in distresses, for Christ's sake. For when I am weak, then I am strong."*

Paul is not looking to look good! He is looking for God to look good. It's not just about the truth we hear but the truth we walk! I embrace my weakness. I don't care what I look like. I care what he looks like. I want his glory, not mine!

Really, Paul has run into the great truth that we must also run into: COMING TO THE END OF YOURSELF. EMBRACING YOUR FRAILTY AND NEEDINESS SO THAT THE GLORY OF GOD CAN BE MADE MANIFEST! This is contrary to our modern thinking and often modern theology, but it is life changing.

If we are to be honest, this truth doesn't work with our modern look-good Christianity, but it works with true Biblical Christianity. Life changing and power of God demonstrating Christianity. Paul came to the Lord with his weakness and came face to face with the grace and glory of God that would change him for the rest of his life. He embraced it, BUT WILL WE, in order to run with the Lord into the fullness of his power and purpose?

CHAPTER 6

The Baptism of The Holy Spirit

It was not too long after I was born again in a Pentecostal church just north of London that I heard this great statement: The baptism of the Holy Spirit. WOW! For a person brought up originally in a traditional church setting this was quite a revelation. The Baptism of the Spirit! This is of course found in Acts 1:5-8. The word baptism has within it the sense of being overwhelmed, meaning something greater and more powerful than yourself whelms you. Jesus actually said,

> *"But you will receive power when the Holy Spirit comes on you…"* Acts 1:8

Power! In the ancient Greek the word is *Dunamis*. A power greater and more overwhelming than ourselves would come upon us and give us divine strength and divine might. Jesus knew what he was prophesying because it had happened to him when that beautiful dove from heaven came upon him.

> *"As soon as Jesus was baptized, he went up out of the water. At that moment heaven was opened, and he saw the Spirit of God descending like a dove and alighting on him."* Matthew 3:16

In fact, a little later he gives a direct quote from Isaiah 61 concerning his baptism:

*"The Spirit of the Lord is upon me, because he has
anointed me to preach the gospel to the poor; he
has sent me to heal the broken hearted, to preach
deliverance to the captives, and recovery of sight to
the blind, to set at liberty them that are oppressed."*
Luke 4:18 NKJV

Oh yes, Jesus who himself had experienced this great
baptism was now prophesying that it was coming upon the
church. Why? Because he was going to send it himself after
his resurrection which Peter later referenced when he said
Jesus had poured out what he had received from the father.
Peter said that this was none other than what the prophet
Joel had meant.

*"Exalted to the right hand of God, he has received
from the Father the promised Holy Spirit and has
poured out what you now see and hear."* Acts 2:33
*"'And afterward,
   I will pour out my Spirit on all people.
Your sons and daughters will prophesy,
   your old men will dream dreams,
   your young men will see visions.'"* Joel 2:28

He was prophesying the great outpouring of the Spirit, this
same baptism. This life changing, power infusing baptism
of the Holy Spirit. Peter himself had now experienced it.
The change was none other than weakness to strength.
Before the baptism he was timid, afraid, keeping his
distance.

The disciples went from a people hiding in an upper room
to a people manifesting God's glory on the street and in the
temple! Why? They had received what Jesus had promised
in Acts 1:5-8. In fact, when Luke recorded the promise he
said Jesus called it power from on high and promised it
would be like being clothed with something that would be
worn from that day on.

*"'I am going to send you what my Father has
promised; but stay in the city until you have been
clothed with power from on high.'"* Luke 24:49

Have you been clothed in such a manner? The promise,
according to Joel, was that it was for all people! This
promise is not just for the select few but all! But then Joel
adds a qualifier in the next verse.

*"'Even on my servants, both men and women,
I will pour out my Spirit in those days.'"*
Joel 2:29

The promise is for all, but all that would serve the living
God. If you have yielded your life to Christ and offered
yourselves as his servants then, like the early disciples and
like multitudes since including me, the baptism of His
Spirit is offered to us and in an ever-increasing measure

according to the depiction of the HOLY SPIRIT in Ezekiel 47:1-6. Realm to realm, depth to depth and strength to strength.

The story of Jabez clearly is one of the shortest and yet most fascinating stories in the Bible. The story is covered in just two verses in 1 Chronicles 4:9-10, yet is so filled with revelation that is none other than a life changer if caught. I first heard someone preach from this passage when I was a young man serving in Bristol in England. The message riveted me! "How did he find that?", I asked myself. It's hidden in all the begats of the verses around it. This gem of truth was there for the searchers to find it. But what a gem! That it is. One of the most classic truths of weakness to strength in the Bible. Let's look at this fascinating story.

Consider the name *Jabez,* the meaning and the curse involved. The meaning of the name *Jabez* is *to grieve on behalf of; sorrowful.*

> *"Jabez was more honorable than his brothers. His mother had named him Jabez, saying, "I gave birth to him in pain."* 1Chronicles 4:9

The meaning of the word translated as *pain* there is also *sorrow.* So, let's look at what she had really named her son: *pain, sorrow and grief.* This clearly had an effect on him because when he came to the Lord for a breakthrough, he says,

"...Let your hand be with me, and keep me from harm so that I will be free from pain."
1 Chronicles 4:10

The naming of him as a child had set a curse upon his life which had deeply affected him and caused him to become the word of the curse.

Now, let's talk about this area of weakness! He was cursed by his own mother with a curse that had an effect that was debilitating, yet there was a great statement in this passage:

"Jabez was more honorable than his brothers."
1 Chronicle 4:9

What does that mean? Mum had obviously done this more than once and the effect on his brothers was that of dishonor clearly both to their mother and seemingly by context to the Lord himself. Not Jabez! No, he acted in honor and it was this act that turned his weakness to strength.

Then came the prayer that changed his life forever. The first thing he did and that we all need to do is involve the Lord. He knew who could change this and knew that if he came in honor that God would act. This is so important to us, whatever our circumstance. Bring in the one who has the power to turn it around. But the words of Jabez' prayer have been one of my favorite sermon topics most of my life. This is his prayer:

"Oh that you would bless me indeed and enlarge my territory and that your hand would be with me, and you would keep me from evil and that I would not cause pain." 1 Chronicles 4:10 NKJV

But the NIV translates the last part, *"so that I will be free from pain."*.

The prayer for blessing was actually twofold:
First, the word *blessing* and the word *indeed* are actually the same Hebrew word. It is the Hebrew word *Bârak* which is actually the same word used to bless God. So now listen to the prayer in a paraphrased manner: Oh that you would bless me, bless me, that it might be a double portion blessing and it would bless others as indeed it will bless you!

The second part is that God would enlarge his territory: that God would increase his measure, his borders and his influence! As David said so long ago:

*"Set me free from my prison,
        that I may praise your name."* Psalm 142:7

Jabez wanted to break out of the limitations of his weakness caused by such a curse! When he asked, "that your hand be with me", he was asking for God's hand of strength, creativity and power! The same hand that would come on Elijah and Elisha and Saul the King. TURN MY WEAKNESS INTO STRENGTH! Then he adds his request to not let that weakness dog him anymore. You know what the scripture says next?

"And God granted his request!" 1 Chronicles 4:10

What brought such a turn around? Honor and the prayer of faith released God's hand to change everything. Do we honor God enough to bring our circumstances to him and, rather than wanting vengeance, seek blessing for the glory of God? Surely this is a wonderful story of weakness to strength. All to the glory of God.

A hidden gem indeed but discoverable for those who want to find the ways of God in men.

CHAPTER 8

The Anointing

One of the greatest verses of the Bible to me is the promise in Isaiah of the anointing that was going to be given to Jesus.

"The Spirit of the sovereign Lord is upon me, because he has anointed me to…" Isaiah 61:1

We are being told that Jesus himself was reliant on the anointing because, even though God in nature, he became a man in function so that the rest of men could potentially walk as he walked. He received the Spirit of the sovereign God, but we receive him as the Spirit of Christ, being sent to us by Christ himself.

"You, however, are not in the realm of the flesh but are in the realm of the Spirit, if indeed the Spirit of God lives in you. And if anyone does not have the Spirit of Christ, they do not belong to Christ." Romans 8:9

"Exalted to the right hand of God, he has received from the Father the promised Holy Spirit and has poured out what you now see and hear." Acts 2:33

What Jesus received he releases to us so that we can in turn function the same way. Jesus received and relied on the anointing which basically means the Holy Spirit's enabling.

The term *anointed to* quoted in Isaiah 61:1 really means *to be enabled to do something that only God the Holy Spirit can enable you to do*.

The word *anointing* means actually *to smear or rub in* as in a manner to become one with you. Somewhat like rubbing cream into the body, it becomes one with you. The anointing becomes one with you and creates an ability to do whatever you are anointed to do. Without it you are in the weakness of the flesh or natural ability but, with it you are enabled by the Most High to administer in a realm that you could never touch in the flesh.

Even though we mention the anointing on Jesus, which to me is the supreme example and the most powerful of all anointings, it is also seen in the Old Testament quite often. It is even recorded of King Saul that he would walk among the prophets and that their anointing would come on him, too. In 1 Samuel 10:5-11, this actually happened twice to him. Elisha was touched by the anointing of Elijah when he cast his mantle upon him in 1 Kings 19:16-19. He later received the fullness of that anointing in 2 Kings 2:12-15. What a powerful impartation of the prophet's anointing. Every king and priest knew of the anointing. Prophets knew of it but one could not speak of the greatness of the anointing without speaking of several outstanding examples. Firstly, David and then the early church. These two are clearly night and day examples. The change and manifestation were as sudden as that!

David

David was anointed in front of his brothers, and it is recorded that the Spirit of the Lord came on him that day.

> *"So Samuel took the horn of oil and anointed him in the presence of his brothers, and from that day on the Spirit of the Lord came powerfully upon David."* 1 Samuel 16:13

From that day things began to change. In fact, people testified to his anointing. It had affected his music, his ability to fight, his valor and his ability to speak. In fact, it is recorded that the Lord was truly with him.

> *"One of the servants answered, 'I have seen a son of Jesse of Bethlehem who knows how to play the lyre. He is a brave man and a warrior. He speaks well and is a fine-looking man. And the Lord is with him.'"* 1 Sam 16:18

This quickly manifests when David faces Goliath! 1 Samuel 17:34-36 he tells the king that he has already defeated lions and bears and Goliath would end up dying to the same anointing. Sure enough, it happened! The power of the anointing! David transformed from a rejected youth in the field to a mighty warrior, worshipper and eventually King! Truly from weakness to strength under the anointing!

The New Testament Church

The promised Holy Spirit fell upon the early church in
according to the promise of Jesus.

> *"All of them were filled with the Holy Spirit and
> began to speak in other tongues[a] as the Spirit
> enabled them."* Acts 2:4

The anointing was so strong that they went from fearful
men to powerful men in a moment! They went from hiding
in an upper room to powerful evangelists and manifestors
of the power of God. The book of Acts is full of what
happened when the anointing hit ordinary men! Church
history is full of the same. Weakness to strength! Fear to
boldness! Enabled by GOD to great feats for him! All
because of the anointing.

The promise wasn't just to a few people but according to
the Prophet Joel it was for all men, young and old and
children, too.

> *"'And afterward,*
> *I will pour out my Spirit on all people.*
> *Your sons and daughters will prophesy,*
> *your old men will dream dreams,*
> *your young men will see visions.'"* Joel 2:28

Actually, Peter quoted Joel in his speech on the day of
Pentecost. This anointing is for all! John speaks of this in
one of his Epistles.

"But you have an anointing from the Holy One, and all of you know the truth." 1 John 2:20

"As for you, the anointing you received from him remains in you, and you do not need anyone to teach you. But as his anointing teaches you about all things and as that anointing is real, not counterfeit—just as it has taught you, remain in him." 1 John 2:27

In fact, in one version it says, "This anointing is real!". It surely is for real! It would take many chapters of this book to speak of all that there is known of the anointing.

The anointing takes us from weakness to strength!

CHAPTER 9

Whose Weakness Was Turned to Strength

This statement is found in Hebrews, but whose weakness was turned to strength? In other words, who was he talking about? This actually gets exciting! He was talking about the multitudes of Old Testament saints both men and women, known and less known who did exploits of faith. A key element in all of them was this: Their weakness was turned to strength!

> *"...who through faith conquered kingdoms, administered justice, and gained what was promised; who shut the mouths of lions, [34] quenched the fury of the flames, and escaped the edge of the sword; whose weakness was turned to strength; and who became powerful in battle and routed foreign armies."* Hebrews 11:33-34

I am sure that if you had told some of them that they were going to be recorded for all to see because of their faith they would have been shocked but indeed there they are. THEY ARE RECORDED FOR US! Normal people. The Lord took their weakness and turned it into a place for his majesty to be revealed! In fact, the Lord in his goodness showed their weaknesses to us so that we could see what he could do with such seemingly unusable people. Then he demonstrates his greatness so that we, too, could hope that he would use us in the same manner. If their weakness was not shown perhaps we would have quickly unlisted ourselves in light of our own glaring weakness!

Weakness? Consider David. He was just a child who was anointed and became a warrior. Or consider Abraham who was enabled to become a father when he was "too old"! Sarah herself was too old but also just didn't believe it was possible. Weakness? Samuel didn't even know God's voice as a child but became one of the greatest prophets of all time. Weakness? What of Rahab the harlot? God used a harlot? Or Samson who lost his strength and eyesight and then in a moment his weakness was turned to strength! The list is endless of both natural and sometimes moral weakness. Some had fear issues and others told lies. Others had anger issues. My point? WEAKNESS! Yes, weakness of all kinds and yet turned to strength when they allowed God to speak and move in their lives.

This list is not just left to Old Testament saints but is found in the New Testament, too. Paul, Peter, Thomas and so the list goes on. It is endless, my friends.

Church history speaks of the same. There have been many whose weaknesses were turned to strength again and again.

What common denominators can be found as we examine these many examples? First, each and every one of them was prepared to own their weakness. We cannot find God's help without being prepared to see the glaring need of it. Paul gets to the place of not only owning his weakness but actually delighting in it.

*"That is why, for Christ's sake, I delight in
weaknesses, in insults, in hardships, in
persecutions, in difficulties. For when I am weak,
then I am strong."* 2 Corinthians 12:10

His statement came after the revelation of the verse before.

*"But he said to me, 'My grace is sufficient for you,
for my power is made perfect in weakness…'."*
2 Corinthians 12:9

Second, looking at Abraham and Paul as examples, is the common denominator of the constant *CALLING ON THE LORD*. This is found throughout their relationships. We so often read that Abraham built an altar and called on the Lord.

*"From there he went on toward the hills east of
Bethel and pitched his tent, with Bethel on the west
and Ai on the east. There he built an altar to
the Lord and called on the name of the Lord."*
Genesis 12:8

Then, of course, is the example of Paul.

*"…I was given a thorn in my flesh, a messenger of
Satan, to torment me. [8] Three times I pleaded with
the Lord to take it away from me."* 2 Corinthians
12: 7-8

A third common denominator would be the receiving of what was given and seeing that it was given as an act of grace and an impartation. Remember what the Lord had said to Paul in 2 Corinthians 12:9. "My grace is sufficient for you." What was the Lord saying? If you want his strength you need to receive his grace. You see, many people who can confess their weakness seem to struggle with the receiving of anything because they miss the grace aspect, of course, coupled with mercy. To receive we must be open to forgiveness and that our weakness opens the door to his greatness.

A fourth common denominator would be having the faith to walk in what the Lord is releasing. As Elisha cried when using the mantle of Elijah the first time,

> *"'Where now is the Lord God of Elijah?'"* 2 Kings 2:14

He had picked up the promised gift, but now was his moment to put it into action. And into action it went! It is recorded of Smith Wigglesworth that when he was forced to pray for his first sick person and left to run his first healing meeting he was thinking that, in his weakness, God would never use him. As he stepped out not knowing but hoping the Lord's hand would be there, BANG, he was shocked as the man was healed! Weakness to strength, indeed. The act of faith in weakness released the greatness of God! Church history is filled with similar stories.

How enthralling that we are found in this great statement, "Whose weakness was turned to strength." In the annals of time and records in heaven, there we will be. Yes, it means me and you!

CHAPTER 10

But David Found Strength In The Lord

WHEN IN DIRE CIRCUMSTANCES

Read 1 Samuel 30:1-6

When we think of Strength coming in weakness we often think of moments of need and encounters in those times of need, but this particular story finds David when he was in the most dire of circumstances. He came home with his fighting men to find his own village attacked, ransacked and burned. His family was gone, taken as slaves. The same had happened to his men. They were broken. In fact, in Verse 4 it is recorded they wept until they could weep no more. Then, on top of that, comes the killer blow. In Verse 6 his men spoke of stoning him as though it was his fault. The scripture records that they were "Bitter in spirit". Gosh, it's hard to fathom such a moment.

Let's then evaluate the situation:

- ❖ They had come home already tired from warfare and skirmishes.

- ❖ Then the shock of seeing their village ransacked and burned.

- ❖ The grief and double shock of their families taken.

- ❖ Then added to this was the worry and stress that their families were either harmed or perhaps dead.

- ❖ Then comes the weeping and grief that wear you out.

- ❖ The terrible sense of responsibility for his men and their loss.

- ❖ Now the men, some of them friends and some of them family, speaking of stoning him.

He was, after all, to blame! Really? These are the times when we need family and friends. Not in this case! The opposite happened. Ever been there? Me too!

Now the situation becomes more shockingly revealing to us. These are the times when many turn tail and run or become angry and incensed or want to give up in despair. But something different happened in David. As he came to absolute brokenness and weakness a supernatural anointing came upon him and he felt the strength of the Lord come up in him. Was it due to his history, his promises or something else? We are not told but suddenly, in a moment, his weakness was turned into strength and he became another man. Had the situation changed? No! BUT HE HAD! That was what mattered. The anointing of strength had been imparted and now the tables were about to turn!

If God can, in a moment, move in such dire circumstances what on earth could he do in our circumstances? Once again another of the patriarchs shows us what an incredible moment it becomes when, in our weakness, his strength is released. These stories are there for our benefit. As one once said, "If he can do it for David, he can do it for me!".

YES, HE CAN! That is the purpose of this book: to release the expectancy and anticipation that our God can take us from weakness to strength.

CHAPTER 11

What Begins as A Decision Becomes A Life Journey

"Blessed are those whose strength is in you, whose hearts are set on pilgrimage." Psalms 84:5

But when we jump forward several verses, we find ourselves in quite a revelation. Just look at the statement,

"They go from strength to strength,
till each appears before God in Zion."
Psalms 84:7

What happens as a decision in verse 5 becomes a lifestyle that takes us from one measure of strength to another. This is particularly hard to grasp in the western world and even more so in the United States where we glorify the strong and the best and the most athletic. We don't even remember the names of the also rans because we like the winner and only the winner. This has been proved just recently when the world-renowned soccer player Lionel Messi began to play in the MLS. Wow, the crowds have started coming to watch in the thousands. With this mentality it is so hard for us to make such a huge decision: THAT WE WILL MAKE GOD OUR STRENGTH. I remember as a young man that I was just like that. I was the only guy in my year at school that played for every school team from soccer to swimming and every other sport, including Rugby. I relied on my physical prowess, my natural toughness and ability. What a journey after I got saved to see that God didn't need my strength but rather, I needed his. Sadly, we often only seem to receive such a revelation after something happens to diminish our natural or mental prowess or when we lose our high paying job. When we are thrown onto the Lord!

There clearly has to be a moment of decision in all of our lives regarding whether we will rely on ourselves and our own prowess or rely on the Lord and his. We are told blessed are they who make the Lord their strength. This decision comes with a preset blessing, but it also comes with a life-changing decision. We either make it be revelation or we make it be circumstances forcing us into a change of view but make it we must. We either rely on us or we let God and all his magnitude and power be our portion.

The second part of Verse 5 shows us that this decision sets us on a journey of discovery and victory and a journey where we see the Lord take us into height after height of who he is and what he can do in us.

The whole context of this revelation is quite amazing. Let's list it:

- ❖ The desire.
  - o *"My soul yearns, even faints, for the courts of the Lord; my heart and my flesh cry out for the living God."* Psalms 84:2

❖ The decision.
  - o *"Blessed are those whose strength is in you, whose hearts are set on pilgrimage."* Psalms 84:5

❖ They pass through trouble.
  - o *"As they pass through the Valley of Baka, [weeping], they make it a place of springs..."* Psalm 84:6

❖ They will increase their strength.
  - o *"They go from strength to strength..."* Psalm 84:7

❖ They find themselves face to face with God.
  - o *"...till each appears before God in Zion."* Psalm 84:7

This is not just a life changer, but it is a game changer! This changes our walk, our relationship and our outcome of life!

CHAPTER 12

The Lesson of The Eagle

One of the greatest lessons of weakness to strength is found in the promises of God for us concerning the eagle. Here are some awesome scriptures:

"Bless the Lord, O my soul,
And forget not all His benefits..."
Psalm 103:2 NKJV

"Who satisfies your mouth with good things,
So that *your youth is renewed like the eagle's."*
Psalm 103:5 NKJV

"But those who wait on the Lord
Shall renew their *strength;*
They shall mount up with wings like eagles,
They shall run and not be weary,
They shall walk and not faint." Isaiah 40:31 NKJV

We as believers are given two great promises. The first is a promise of the benefits for those who belong to God! TO BE RENEWED LIKE AN EAGLE! A fair question is, "How is an eagle renewed?". The second promise also speaks of renewal and is that of renewal of strength which causes us to fly in the heights.

What is so great in these promises is the work of the Holy Spirit and how he helps us. Just as the eagle is renewed so are we! The Holy Spirit is the renewer. The scripture speaks of the renewing of the Holy Spirit.

> *"He saved us through the washing of rebirth and renewal by the Holy Spirit..."* Titus 3:5

The word *renew* has within it the sense of *renovation* which means *to make as if it were brand new; as at the beginning.* The eagle is renowned for having its plumage and its beak renewed so that it can soar and hunt again. We are renewed so that we can flow, minister and catch the winds of the Spirit again. However, the Isaiah passage brings us into involvement in this process. Those that wait on, hope in and become entangled with the Lord will renew our strength. The Holy Spirit works renewal within us but we fall on him and become entangled with him. We, like the eagle, need renewing. The illustration is amazing! What better typology is there? Is there anything as magnificent as an eagle in the air? And to compare us to such a magnificent bird, what a heavenly illustration! We, too, become magnificent when we are renewed in the Spirit realm.

- ❖ A renewed eagle can soar above the storm.

- ❖ A renewed eagle can see its prey over a mile away.

- ❖ A renewed eagle can climb to great heights.

- ❖ A renewed eagle can catch the winds as it spreads out its magnificent plumage.

- ❖ A renewed eagle can fly at great speeds.

The comparison is wonderful:

- ❖ A renewed person can rise above the storms of life.

- ❖ A renewed person can envision all the Lord wants them to see. The Scripture in jumps to mind:
    - o *"Your eyes will see the king in his beauty and view a land that stretches afar."* Isaiah 33:17

- ❖ A renewed person can move with *hinds' feet.*
    - o *"He makes my feet like the feet of a deer; he causes me to stand on the heights."* Psalm 18:33
    - o *"The Lord God is my strength, and he will make my feet like hinds' feet, and he will make me to walk upon mine high places."* Habakkuk 3:19. KJV.
    - o *"...they are the ones who will dwell on the heights, whose refuge will be the mountain fortress. Their bread will be supplied, and water will not fail them."* Isaiah 33:16

- ❖ A renewed person is a person of the Spirit, able to flow with and walk with the Holy Spirit in all ways and open to his voice and promptings.

- ❖ A renewed person can run under the anointing and not grow weary.

- o   *"They will soar on wings like eagles;*
    they will run and not grow weary,
    they will walk and not be faint."
  Isaiah 40:31
- o   *"The power of the Lord came on Elijah and,*
    tucking his cloak into his belt, he ran ahead
    of Ahab all the way to Jezreel."
  1 Kings 18:46
  HE OUTRAN A CHARIOT!

So, weakness to strength includes the work of renewal both internally and physically, so that YOUR youth will be renewed like the eagle!

CHAPTER 13

The Holy Spirit Helps Us in Our Weakness

What a statement! In fact, this verse is the key verse to our whole revelation, it makes us aware of much of his personal function to us.

> *"In the same way, the Spirit helps us in our weakness."* Romans 8:26

> *"'And I will ask the Father, and he will give you another advocate to help you and be with you forever—'"* John 14:16

Jesus had promised us that the Paraclete was coming to replace him in person. One of the meanings of the word *Paraclete* is *one drawn alongside to help.* But our promise is not just to be helped but that he would help us in our weaknesses!

Now, here comes the amazing revelation: the meaning of the word *weakness*! In the original Greek it means *frailty of mind and of body; frailty morally and fiscally.* It covers every kind of weakness! This is the same word used when The Lord tells Paul that his strength (Dunamis) is made perfect in our weakness. This is a game changer and a mind blower! Our religious minds want to condemn us for our weakness, but the Bible says that the Holy Spirit was sent to help us in the very weakness that religion would love to condemn!

Now let's look at what the word *help* means. It is only used twice in the New Testament and means *to assist; co-operate; to hold two opposites together.* HE HELPS JOIN THE BROKEN PARTS! He assists like one helping us on crutches and works alongside like an aid. Whatever the weakness, he is there to restore and help. Perhaps we could look at a listing of some of the places where this could operate:

- ❖ When we can't pray right.

    - o *"...We do not know what we ought to pray for, but the Spirit himself intercedes for us through wordless groans."* Romans 8:26

- ❖ When we are in a terrible warfare.

    - o *"'My grace is sufficient for you, for my power is made perfect in weakness.'"* 2 Corinthians 12:9

- ❖ When we trip up. (Guess who his hand is!)

    - o *"The Lord makes firm the steps of the one who delights in him; ²⁴ though he may stumble, he will not fall, for the Lord upholds him with his hand."* Psalms 37:23-24

- ❖ When we walk in the valley of trouble.
    - o *"Even though I walk through the darkest valley,*

❖ When we need our inner man strengthened.

  o *"Now to him who is able to do immeasurably more than all we ask or imagine, according to his power that is at work within us…"* Ephesians 3:20

❖ When we need our soul restored.

  o *"He makes me lie down in green pastures, he leads me beside quiet waters, he refreshes my soul."* Psalms 23:2-3

❖ When we need comforting.

  o *"…he will give you another advocate to help you and be with you forever."* John 14:16 Paraclete also means comforter.

❖ When we need healing.

  o *"And the power of the Lord was with Jesus to heal the sick."* Luke 5:17

These are but a few examples. The list is immense and the more you study it, the more stirred you become! He is here to help, whatever the weakness or circumstance. Perhaps one of the most moving scriptures of all concerning the ministry of Jesus (it is he who released the Holy Spirit among us after all) is in Hebrews. Whatever version you read it has the same application, so let's quote the NKJV.

Quite simply, it touches him. So, his answer? Sending and releasing the Holy Spirit to help us.

CHAPTER 14

Being Brought Into A Place Of Weakness

We have seen how the Lord brought Paul, a man of great intellect and great faith, to a place of weakness so that the power of God could be made manifest. We have seen it also with Abraham, Caleb and in so many in the Bible. How does God get us to such a place that we can no longer rely on ourselves, but our heart turns to the Lord for our strength? Well, the list is numerous, but the ways of God are always the same. Here are a few of those ways:

- ❖ Failure. Peter is a great example of this. His failure both in the garden and during Jesus' trial brought him to a place of being able to receive such might on the day of Pentecost.

- ❖ Brokenness. David, after his brokenness, found the Lord in a new way!

- ❖ Brought to weakness physically. Abraham of course and Jacob in Genesis 32.

- ❖ When nothing works. Paul with the thorn in the flesh and Peter when he goes fishing in John 21.

- ❖ Circumstances beyond your control. Here we have Jabez and the woman with the issue of blood as prime examples. One cursed by a mother and another a physical sickness and loss of finances.

These examples are not all because sometimes it comes by another way such as:

- ❖ Revelation. Where God imputes his knowledge to you that changes the way you see things. Paul speaks of it in Ephesians 1:17-19. Abraham was also told that what he saw would change what he believed and walked in Genesis 13:14.

- ❖ Encounter. When the Lord touches you supernaturally, either sovereignly or through a man. Both Paul and Elisha experienced these aspects.

- ❖ Discipleship. Learning from others who have walked before you and learning by their experiences. I know I have been constantly affected by others.

These are just a few of the ways of God to bring us to reliance. The sooner they're learned the better and the greater the potential of his greatness being manifested in our lives.

"Lift up your heads, O you gates!
And be lifted up, you everlasting doors!
And the King of glory shall come in."
Psalms 24:7 NKJV

Lord let us see it, that we might partake of it!

When Paul wrote to the Philippians, as in all his epistles, he spoke not just from revelation but personal experience. There are so many amazing gems in this particular epistle, but one verse of his personal experience is so important to this book concerning weakness to strength.

"I can do all things through Christ who strengthens me.' Philippians" 4:13 NKJV

Paul, who had experienced that great revelation in 2 Corinthians, concerning that in our weakness his strength is perfected, now gives us his actual life walk! There is nothing I can't do if I rely on the strength of the Lord. If I recognize my frailty and rely on his strength, there is no arena it does not operate in. IN ALL THINGS, CHRIST CAN AND DOES STRENGTHEN ME. It means there is no arena in my life it doesn't work if I learn the lesson of reliance. This indeed gives the whole purpose of our book. Such great purpose! It works in every area! Paul had experienced it and is now telling us we can, too. How many times have we felt that we have been dropped into something beyond our experience or beyond our depth to swim? How many challenges do we face both natural and spiritual? How often are we sent to do a task seemingly too difficult or are prompted beyond our ability? Well, here is our promise: I can do all things through Christ Jesus who strengthens me.

Abraham, Jabez, David, Paul and many others are there to show that this truth is really a truth! It's not just a thought but a reality. This truth is ours to see and gain and walk. It has become mine more and yet more. Now let it become yours too. HIS STRENGTH IS PERFECTED IN OUR WEAKNESS AND ALL AREAS ARE COVERED!

"From Weakness to Strength.

I can't think of a more relevant message for the body of Christ than this latest offering from Dennis Goldsworthy—Davis. From *Weakness to Strength* is a masterful journey through Scripture with an understanding of its practical application. Dennis's life journey is that of a man who understands that without HIS strength, we cannot fulfill the purpose for which we are called. What you have in your hand is more than a how-to 'get by' in the face of difficulty or how to muster enough strength to complete your next ministry assignment. As Dennis weaves Scripture around his personal testimony of over fifty years in ministry, one begins to sense that this book is more than something to read, but something to live! I highly recommend you buy two copies of this book…one for you and one for a friend who may need encouragement to "press on toward the goal for the prize of the upward call of God in Christ Jesus!"

J. Tod Zeiger
todzeiger@gmail. com
San Antonio, Texas

"I met Dennis at Peterborough Bible Week many years ago. During the years that I have known Dennis, not only is he a great friend and man of God, but the prophetic apostolic calling on his life is unique. This incisive, accurate, biblical, prophetic gift not only changes people's lives, but brings tremendous biblical guidance to the government of any local church. Both my wife and I highly recommend Dennis' ministry to any emerging apostolic leadership, local church pastors, and to all those that have a heart of the kingdom. He has been invaluable to the life of our church and our people."   -Steve Maile

"This message comes from a very grateful heart ... a couple years ago, my husband Theo and I were attending Oasis and Pastor Dennis prayed for us to have a baby and prophesied that he could see it growing in my womb. I had a struggle with my faith as we had been trying to conceive for several years without success and I was starting to give up hope. But knowing that God isn't a liar, we held fast to that word, and this month we welcomed our little baby girl, Karina Luna. Thank you for praying for us and releasing faith into our lives and serving as a voice for God's promise. God bless you!"   -Kat S.

"Awesome time (Friday Night, Saturday morning) with Dennis Goldsworthy-Davis. Have not experienced manifestations of the Holy Spirit like that before!! Looking forward to more renewal, revival, restoration Hosea 6:1-3. Bring it on!" -Nigel Reid

Dennis Paul Goldsworthy-Davis has been blessed to travel extensively throughout the world ministering both apostolically and prophetically to the body of Christ. He operates within a strong governmental prophetic office and frequently sees the Presence of God and the Spirit of Revival break out upon the lives of people. Dennis has equally been graced to relate to many spiritual sons throughout the earth, bringing wisdom, guidance and encouragement.

Born in Southern Ireland and raised in England, Dennis was radically saved from a life of drugs and violence in 1973. Soon after his conversion, he began to operate within his local church where he was fathered spiritually by Bennie Finch, a seasoned apostolic minister. After working in youth ministry Dennis pastored in several areas within the U.K. It was during these pastorates that Dennis began to see profound moves of God in these same venues.

In 1986 Dennis experienced a dramatic shift in his life and ministry. He and his family moved to San Antonio, Texas, to join a vibrant, functioning apostolic team. In 1990 Dennis was commissioned to start Great Grace International Christian Center, a local work in San Antonio. Dennis continues to serve as the Senior Minister of GGICC and heads the formation of the apostolic team in the local house. Presently, Dennis relates to several functioning apostolic ministries. He draws wisdom and accountability

from Robert Henderson of Global Reformers, Barry
Wissler of HarvestNet International and for many years,
Alan Vincent. Each of these carry strong, well-seasoned
apostolic offices in their own right.

Dennis has been married to his wife, Christine, since 1973
and has two wonderful daughters and four grandchildren.

Printed in Dunstable, United Kingdom

65095241R00040